Change Makers

Written by Libby Martinez

Acknowledgments

The publisher would like to thank the following for their kind permission to reproduce their photographs:

(Key: b-bottom; c-center; l-left; r-right; t-top)

123RF.com: 1b, Boris Sosnovyy 17b, Cathy Yeulet 30b, Kjersti Jorgensen 15, Markus Mainka 22-23; **Alamy Images:** Bernd Mellman 12b, Bernhard Classen 8, Blend Images 10-11c, Charles Sturge 9, David Grossman 26br, Doug Webb 21cr, Eve Edelheit / Tampa Bay Times / ZUMAPRESS.com 22, F1online digitale Bildagentur GmbH 25, Fabian von Poser 6-7, FBI Photo 20-21, Florian Kopp / imageBROKER 4r, Hero Images inc 5t, Hill Street Studios / Eric Raptosh / Blend Images 27t, 28t, Jeff Greenberg 18br, JeffreyIsaacGreenberg 31, Kees Metselaar 14-15, Kidstock / Blend Images 24, Lee Karen Stow 8bl, Myrleen Pearson 23t, 29tl, 29b, Paula Solloway 11t, 25tr, 26tl, Peter Hermes Furian 7b, 13b, Richard Whitcombe 16b, RosaIreneBetancourt 3 27bl, Wenn Ltd 12t; **Corbis:** Kidstock / Blend Images 24tr; **Getty Images:** Gordon Chibroski / Portland Press Herald 28b, Joey Foley / WireImage for Philanthropy Project 18tl, John Lamparski / Wireimage 6tl, Win McNamee 19tr; **Shutterstock.com:** Depiano 3, 5tr, 7cr, 9c, 11c, 12c, 15c, 16c, 19c, 20c, 21c, 23c, 24c, 25t, 26c, 27b, 28c, 29c, 30c, design56 20cl, f9photos 20tl, Patryk Kosmide 26, photosync 20tr, Vladislav Gurfinkel 19b

Cover images: *Front:* **Alamy Images:** Hill Street Studios / Eric Raptosh / Blend Images; *Back:* **123RF.com**

All other images © Pearson Education

Picture Research by: Susie Prescott

Every effort has been made to trace the copyright holders and we apologize in advance for any unintentional omissions. We would be pleased to insert the appropriate acknowledgment in any subsequent edition of this publication.

ISBN-13: 978-0-328-83282-8
ISBN-10: 0-328-83282-0

5 6 7   18 17 16

Contents

Can You Make Change Happen?

Young people around the world are solving problems. They work hard to make their neighborhoods better. Are you creative and smart? Do you work hard? Do you never give up? If so, you can make change happen!

Ideas + Action = Change

Every change starts with an idea. People think of ideas to solve problems. They think of ways to make the world better. Some people like to invent machines. Others like helping plants and animals. Some help people who have been hurt by disasters.

This boy is helping his community by planting trees.

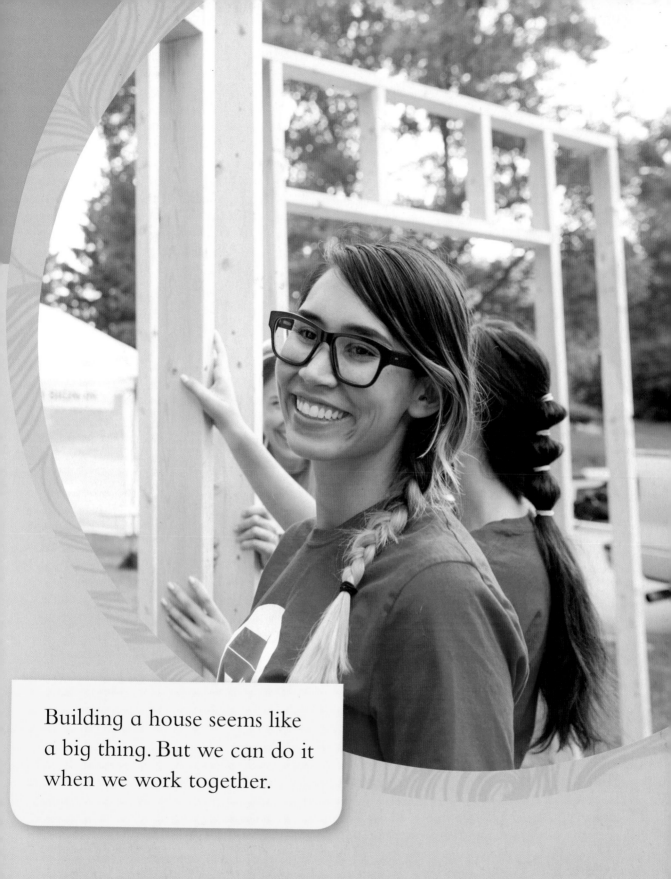

Building a house seems like a big thing. But we can do it when we work together.

Let's meet some young people who are changing the world!

Kelvin Doe

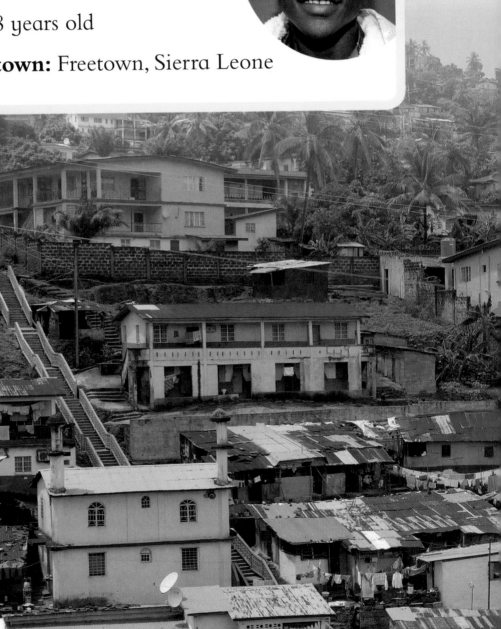

Change Maker

Name: Kelvin Doe

Age: 18 years old

Hometown: Freetown, Sierra Leone

Kelvin Doe is an inventor. He taught himself how to make things. When he was ten years old, Kelvin wanted to help people. He started to think of ideas. Kelvin thought about problems in his neighborhood. There was a lack of electricity. The lights only came on once a week. Kelvin had an idea to help the lights stay on!

Fact File

Sierra Leone

Location: Sierra Leone is a country in West Africa.

Population: More than five million people

Capital: Freetown

Climate: Tropical

FREETOWN

S I E R R A   L E O N E

Lights On!

Kelvin's family could not afford batteries. The lights needed batteries to work. Kelvin wanted to fix the problem. He started collecting electronic parts that people had thrown away. Kelvin used the parts to make a battery when he was thirteen years old. Now Kelvin's batteries power lights all over his neighborhood!

Cell Phone Power

Kelvin kept thinking of ideas to help. His next invention was a generator. It charged batteries. His neighbors needed these batteries to charge their cell phones.

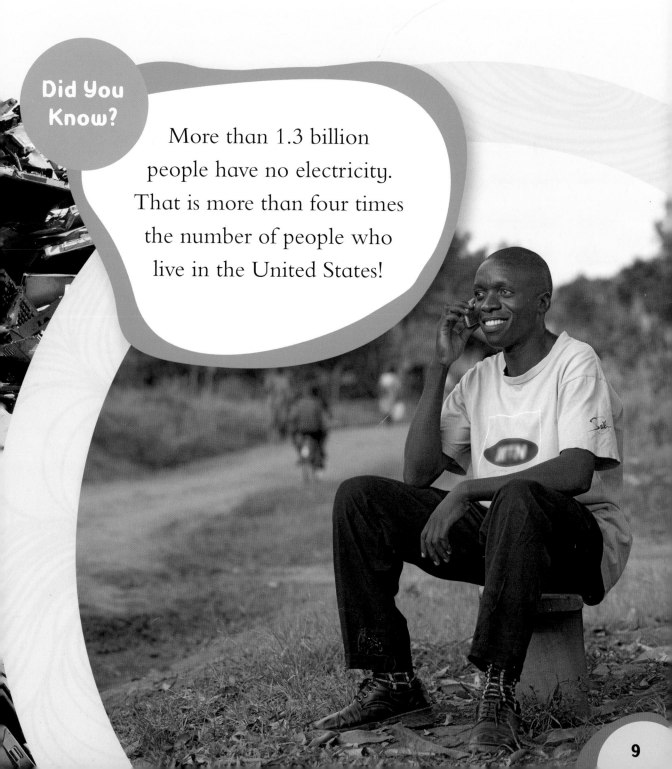

Did You Know?

More than 1.3 billion people have no electricity. That is more than four times the number of people who live in the United States!

Future Plans

Kelvin keeps inventing and working on ideas. One of his new projects is building a windmill. The windmill will provide power to his neighborhood. He is also working on a solar power project. The project will power computers. Students can use these computers to go on the Internet.

Solar panels collect energy from the Sun. The energy is used to make electricity.

Old packaging can be used in many different ways.

What Can You Do?

Be creative like Kelvin! Reuse items to help solve problems. Don't throw away plastic bottles. Use them to make bird feeders. This will help wildlife in your neighborhood.

Madison Vorva and Rhiannon Tomtishen

Change Makers

Names: Madison Vorva and Rhiannon Tomtishen

Ages: 19 years old

Hometown: Ann Arbor, Michigan

Madison and Rhiannon have tried to help orangutans like this one.

Madison and Rhiannon have been working to change the world. When they were both eleven years old, they were Girl Scouts. They decided to earn a Girl Scout Bronze Award. To earn the award, they learned about endangered orangutans.

Orangutans

There are two types of orangutans. They come from the islands of Sumatra and Borneo. They are called Sumatran and Bornean orangutans.

Sumatra

Borneo

INDIAN OCEAN

JAVA SEA

Java

Bali

Palm Oil

Madison and Rhiannon learned that orangutans live in the rain forest. They discovered that the orangutans' homes were being destroyed. Trees were being chopped down so that palm oil plants could be grown. Palm oil is used in products such as candy bars, cookies, and shampoo.

Taking Action!

Madison and Rhiannon checked which products used palm oil. They discovered that palm oil was an ingredient in Girl Scout cookies. The girls decided to take action. They wanted the cookies to be made without harming the rain forest. By protecting the forest they could help the orangutans.

Did You Know?

There are fewer than 7,500 Sumatran orangutans left in the wild. If we keep destroying their habitat, they could become extinct.

Letters and E-mails

Madison and Rhiannon asked people to write e-mails to the Girl Scout headquarters. The e-mails asked for the cookies to be made without destroying the rain forest. People sent 70,000 e-mails! Now the makers of many of the cookies do not harm the rain forest. In 2012, Rhiannon and Madison received the first-ever United Nations Forest Heroes Award.

Did You Know?

There are more than 2 million homeless children in the United States.

Many homes were destroyed by Hurricane Katrina.

Guinness World Record

Zach always has new ideas. In 2014, he helped collect more than 500,000 pounds of food. The food was given to families in need. The food weighed as much as 37 elephants! He collected all of the food in 24 hours. This set a new world record. Zach never stops trying to make the world a better place.

In 2013, Zach stayed in a box for seven days. Cans of food were donated to cover the walls of the box. The food was given to those in need.

What Can You Do?

If a disaster happens, there are many ways to help. Collect supplies such as water, blankets, and clothing. You can also collect canned food. Give these items to victims of the disaster.

Kids to the Rescue!

Sometimes adults need kids to help take action. Just like you, these adults want to make the world better. Many of them have already started projects in your community. But they need hardworking kids like you!

Community Gardens

Around the world, people are planting gardens and trees in their communities. Community gardens create habitats for animals. They also provide fresh fruits and vegetables. These can be given to families who don't have enough food. Adults need kids to help plant seeds and water the gardens.

Eating fresh fruits and vegetables helps people stay healthy.

Bradford Community Garden

Location: Bradford, West Yorkshire (United Kingdom)

Facts: Kids learn about healthy eating and growing food in this garden. They also learn about nature and the environment.

Brightmoor Youth Garden

Location: Detroit, Michigan

Facts: Brightmoor Youth Garden is a community garden just for kids. Kids learn how to grow and harvest vegetables there.

Community Art

Do you like to paint? Find out about art projects in your community. There might be some that you could help work on. Sometimes community groups create colorful murals. These can brighten up neighborhood buildings.

Fact File

HandsOn Miami

Location: Miami, Florida

Facts: HandsOn Miami has lots of projects that kids can help with. They made this mural to decorate a school.

27

Community Champions

Making the world better takes people. It also takes hard work. There are lots of community projects that need people's help. They need people like you!

Community projects can help you meet new people.

Community projects can help you learn new skills.

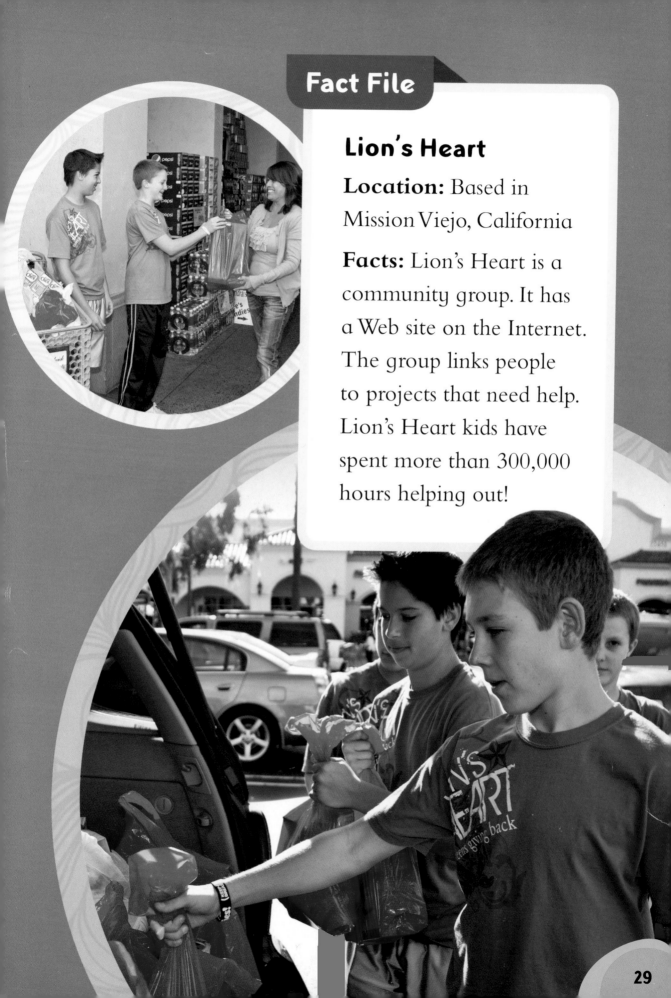

Lion's Heart

Location: Based in Mission Viejo, California

Facts: Lion's Heart is a community group. It has a Web site on the Internet. The group links people to projects that need help. Lion's Heart kids have spent more than 300,000 hours helping out!

Are you ready to start changing the world? Follow these four steps to make the world a better place.

Step 1:

Think of a problem you would like to solve.

Step 2:

Be creative! List ideas for solving that problem.

Step 3:

Turn your ideas into action. You can do this on your own or with a friend. You can also join a group that is trying to solve the same problem.

Step 4:

Work hard! Never give up! The world needs you.

Glossary

climate   the type of weather a place usually has

creative   able to think of new ideas for solving problems

extinct   no longer existing

generator   machine that can produce electrical energy

mural   large painting on a wall or building

solar power   energy from the Sun that is converted into electricity

United Nations   international organization that promotes peace and cooperation around the world

Index